# Your Best Business Card

## How to Stand Out

## from the Competition

## with Your Very Own Book

by

Ida Shessel

Published by Lindmaur Publishing, a division of Ida Shessel International, Inc.

www.LindmaurPublishing.com

ISBN  978-0-9920887-6-7


Shessel, Ida

Your Best Business Card:  How to Stand Out from the Competition with Your Very Own Book

Warning – Disclaimer

# Table of Contents

Chapter 1: The Typical Business Card...................................1

Networking Events ...................................2

But My Card is Different ...................................3

Meeting with Prospects ...................................6

What's the Solution to this Problem? ...................................7

Chapter 2: Your Best Business Card...................................9

You're a Celebrity ...................................10

Books Garner Respect ...................................10

Prospecting...................................11

What Your Book Will and Won't Do...................................12

Pushing Past Your Barriers ...................................13

Chapter 3: Your Marketing Advantage...................................19

What are Your Competitors Doing? ...................................19

You and Your Competitors are Fighting Over the Same Group of Prospects...................................20

What's Your Approach? ...................................23

So How Do You Educate Them? ...................................24

What Influences Your Prospects' Decision to Buy a Product or Service? ...................................25

Your Book Can Make the Difference........................................30

Chapter 4: Getting Started on Your Book ..................................33

Narrowing Down the Expertise You Want to Promote........33

Selecting Your Target Market........................................34

Determining Your Objective ....................................35

Deciding on the Style of Your Book............................37

Chapter 5: Writing Your Book........................................39

Creating a Benefit-Oriented Title ............................39

Compiling the Content for Your Book........................41

Credibility Enhancers ............................................45

Chapter 6: Preparing your Book for Print Publication..............47

Interior Decisions ....................................................48

Exterior Cover Design........................................49

Publishing to Amazon's CreateSpace........................50

The Approval Process ............................................51

Chapter 7: Your Next Step ..........................................55

Our Services ........................................................57

About the Author ..................................................59

Testimonials..............................................................61

Other Books by Ida Shessel........................................63

# Chapter 1:

# The Typical Business Card

Do you have a business card? You probably do. Who doesn't these days?

What does your business card look like? The standard 2 by 3.5 inch card doesn't really have room for very much, but I'll hazard a guess that either you or a designer spent considerable time trying to design the perfect business card.

But what does your business card do for you?

## Networking Events

Imagine yourself at a networking event or a "business card exchange". You're either mingling with the crowd or you're sitting around a table at a breakfast or lunch meeting introducing yourself to 6 or 7 other people. You hand out your business card and receive others in return. Later on when you get back to the office, you pull out all the business cards you collected – and do what?

One possibility is that you or your assistant enters all the information into your contact management system. Another even stronger possibility is that you leave the business cards on the corner of your desk until you have a chance to look at them later. If and when you actually get around to looking at each card, you'll probably be at a total loss trying to remember the person who gave it to you. What did that person look like? What was the conversation you had with him or her? What was memorable about that person? More importantly, what is that person's expertise? How do you know? Chances are you can't remember, so you toss the card into the "circular file" (also known as the trash can). The same happens with the next and the next and the next card until you've scooped up all of them and sent them the way of the first.

## But My Card is Different

You may be thinking "No one is going to throw my card away. Mine's different." Is it? Do you really think that the people you've met at all those networking events are doing anything differently with the card you gave them?

Did you truly make a positive impression on the people you exchanged business cards with? There probably wasn't time, because after all, you were only with them a few short minutes before you moved on to the next person. What made you stand out in the minds of those you met? What made you memorable? Will that business card get you more clients?

If you're a realtor, there probably were other realtors in the room. If you're an accountant, there probably were other accountants in the room. If you're a financial advisor or lawyer or website developer, there probably were other financial advisors or lawyers or website developers in the room. How did you stand out from those who do what you do? I could go on, but you get the picture.

Why should someone looking for your service choose you over any of the others they've met?

If I've met three bankers or estheticians or chiropractors in the last little while, and I don't have a recommendation from a friend, how do I choose one when I need one? Why should I choose you? If your answer is "I have lots of experience. I've been in business for 20 years," I'm about to burst your bubble – and you might take offense at what I'm about to say...but longevity doesn't tell me anything about your expertise, your credibility, or your success. It just means that you've run the marathon.

I've been to many networking events and one of the things that I always hear from accountants is "I can save you taxes." Well, if I've met three accountants at the event, which one do I choose if I want to save taxes? What sets one apart from the other? I'm not picking on accountants, by the way. My husband is an accountant and in a former lifetime, I was an accounting student. This is just an illustration of how necessary it is to find a way to stand out from the competitors in your marketplace.

The exchange of business cards has become a mindless ritual in the same way as "Hi, how are you?" has become. There is no thought as to how effective it is.

Your business card doesn't do you or your expertise any justice. It doesn't tell prospective clients what you can do for them – nor does it instantly provide value or establish credibility. In most cases, your business card doesn't give the receiver a reason to call you. Even a line such as "call for a free quote or consultation" isn't a strong enough call to action for most people. Many are reluctant to call for fear of being pressured or harassed into buying. They are afraid of getting stuck in a business relationship they can't get out of, so they don't call even if your product or service is what they need. They're already anticipating the discomfort they are going to feel if it turns out that the product or service isn't a fit for them and they need to decline your offer. And so they remain unaware of your expertise.

## Meeting with Prospects

Recently I met an osteopath/massage therapist at a networking event. His professional combination is not one that I come across every day, and there are probably others just like me who are unsure of what he does and why they (or others they can refer) might need his services. He has developed methods that differentiate his approach to pain management from that of other practitioners. Yet, how does this osteopath/massage therapist let others know how his approach differs from conventional therapies and how his patients have benefited? He is probably finding it necessary to explain his services over and over and over again – and unless people take a chance and give his services a try, they may never know.

Here's another scenario. Imagine you have a meeting scheduled with a prospective client and plan on walking him/her through a "pitch" of your products and services. Your prospect has already met with one of your competitors and is planning to meet with another one in a few days. In your prospect's mind, there may not be much of a difference between what you have to offer and what the others have to offer. You need to differentiate yourself and stand out in some way. What can you do proactively to increase the possibility that you'll be hired and eventually referred by this prospect?

## So What's the Solution to this Problem?

Is the solution a jazzier business card? Is it a great graphic or photo on your business card? Is it a snappy line when you approach people? Should you wear a clown's nose and hat at the next networking event you attend? What will set you apart and give others a way to get to know your expertise quickly and memorably?

The solution is complex and may include elements such as branding, marketing, pricing, a confident demeanor, a well-worded pitch, and so on.

This book deals with one solution that has two elements I think you're going to like. It's fairly quick, and it elevates you in the eyes of your prospect.

# Chapter 2:

## Your Best Business Card

What will position you as an expert, help you stand out from the competition in your market place, and get you more clients? The answer to that is something a whole lot better than a 2 by 3.5 inch piece of light card stock.

It's a book -- not just any book, but *your* book.

I'm talking here, by the way, about a physical book -- not an e-book. I'm talking about a softcover or hardcover book – something that has "thud" factor.

What's thud factor? Here, try this. Take this book (but mark this page first so you can come back and continue reading). Toss it on a table. What sound do you hear?

Thud! Every book makes that sound. The more substantial the book, the louder or deeper the thud – and the more impressive it is. Compare that to an ordinary business card!

## You're a Celebrity!

Imagine yourself handing your book to a prospect. I've done it many times and the reaction from the other person is always surprise and delight. They're impressed. "Oh, you've written a book!" They tend to attribute all sorts of characteristics to you – that you're an authority; that you're particularly gifted, educated, and intelligent; that you're a skilled writer/communicator, and even that you're a celebrity.

To most people, writing and publishing a book is a mysterious undertaking – one that they feel is beyond their ability. (Let this be our little secret:  it's easier and faster than they think!)

## Books Garner Respect

When you receive a book from someone, would you consider throwing it into the trash as you would a business card? No. Books are revered. Chances are high that you aren't going to toss it into the circular file. Even if you decide not to read it, you'll most likely look for something more respectful to do with it. You'll put it on your desk or your book shelf, display it in your reception area, give it away to a colleague or a friend, donate it to a library or a charity, or sell it at a garage sale -- almost anything except throw it away.

## Prospecting

Your book gives your prospects much more than just the contact information found on a business card. Compared to your competition, you're ahead out of the starting gate because you're giving them a chance to get to know you and you don't need to be "selling", connecting by telephone or Skype, or physically meeting with them to do that – yet. You're already beginning to gain their trust and fuel their desire to work with you and your business. And all without pressure.

A great advantage to having a book is that your prospects and clients can re-read your book as many times as they like. What a great way to have your message repeated, strengthened, and remembered! You did the work once and it can continue to reap rewards for you for a long time after. Even better, your readers can pass your book along to others and you get new sources of exposure and referrals.

## What Your Book Will and Won't Do

Let's be honest. Your book won't instantly get you sales. What it will do is pre-sell you. What do I mean? Well, let me put it this way. Even before you have any conversations with your prospects, your book gives them an opportunity to get to know you and your expertise. Your book can help them gain a perspective on how you approach your work – your philosophy, your attitude, and your methods. Even the tone of your book speaks to them in a particular way – giving them a flavor for your personality, approachability, formality, and sense of humor (if any). Examples specific to your industry and your clients help them determine if you're a good fit for their needs.

My former business coach James Malinchak (featured on the ABC television network's show Secret Millionaire) always insists that his coachees write a book as the very first marketing piece they create before anything else. He says it positions you, the writer, as an expert. James often tells the story of how he found his current dentist because of his book. Dr. Bill Dorfman is known as the dentist to the stars and was the dentist on ABC's Extreme Makeover and CBS' The Doctors. He wrote a book called *Billion Dollar Smile: A Complete Guide to Your Extreme Smile Makeover*. The book was displayed in a number of different offices and eventually James saw it, picked it up, read it, and went in search of Dr. Bill's services. In addition to this being the beginning of a dentist/patient relationship, James and Dr. Bill also developed a philanthropic relationship in that James continues to be a generous contributor to Dr. Bill's youth leadership foundation. You just never know how far your book might travel and who might see it.

## Pushing Past Your Barriers

So, you don't think you could write a book? The following are four of the most common concerns I hear.

**Concern #1: I'm not a writer. I could never write a book.**

You are an experienced professional. Perhaps you also have various certifications, degrees, or diplomas. You have knowledge and experience that can help others. Even if you have less-than-terrific writing skills and think you can't write a book, I guarantee you that you can "talk" a book. You communicate with prospects and clients all the time – talking about the very same things that can be turned into a book. All you need is some guidance and coaching to draw out and record the content in an organized fashion. Once the main topics are outlined, it's just a matter of fleshing them out with explanations and examples and then polishing them up.

**Concern #2: Writing and publishing a book takes so long. It's a daunting task and very intimidating.**

It can be done faster than you can imagine! Luckily there are publishers who are expert at the entire process from start to finish. Lindmaur Publishing can assist you in getting your book from your head to your hands very quickly.

**Concern #3: I don't like rejection.**

Who does? Imagine putting your heart and soul into your manuscript and submitting it to a publisher only to have it come back to you with a politely worded rejection. You're crushed – discouraged.

Rejection generally comes from the big publishing houses that are looking for viable best sellers (read that as big $$$ $) for their business. They are inwardly focused on their bottom line.

Our approach eliminates rejection. Lindmaur Publishing is outwardly focused. We're in business to help you and your business look good – establish credibility, authority, and respect. We want to help you create something better than a business card to hand out when you're marketing. We're not about creating bestsellers. Our purpose is to assist you in writing and publishing your book (and getting it up on Amazon, if that's what you want as well).

**Concern #4:   If I put what I know in a book, no one will buy my product or service.**

The way I see it, there will always be five different groups of people who read your book.

People in group one will read your book but do nothing with what they read. The second group consists of those who go off after reading your book and implement the ideas themselves (if your topic lends itself to this). Group three is composed of those who source the expertise elsewhere (not from you). Those in the fourth group want to know what needs to be done but are willing to have you, the expert, do it. The last group just wants to see the end result and is more than willing to give the project over to you to take care of all the details of "the what and how". You can't do anything about the first three groups -- and really, there won't be all that many of them. Just let them go and focus on groups four and five.

Remember that the idea here is not to create a comprehensive document of everything you know about your area of expertise. You're writing a book in order to position yourself as the best seller of your particular product or service. You want to talk about *what* you do, not *how* you do it. You want to answer "frequently asked questions" and "should ask questions" (more about those later) as well as give examples of client problems you've solved.

One last thing: Depending on your area of expertise, there will also be people who want other products or services from you that you may not have addressed in your book but have mentioned during conversations or presentations, on your website, or in your other marketing materials. Your book lays the groundwork for these as well.

Let's move on and have a look at the marketing benefits your book will give you.

# Chapter 3:

# Your Marketing Advantage

## What are Your Competitors Doing?

As you look around and study experts within your field, what do you notice? What's different about them versus you? What seemingly unfair advantage do they have? Generally, they find ways to be seen and heard – through their books, the media, and speaking engagements. These strategies create the image or perception of being "bigger" in the mind of prospects.

You can start with something small that looks big in the eyes of your prospects. A book creates a great first impression – and it's one that gives you a fair advantage. Most business people haven't written a book. But if *you* do,

it will provide you with instant credibility and authority –
and a distinct marketing advantage.

## You and Your Competitors are Fighting Over the Same Group of Prospects

Consider this. Let's assume that you are targeting one
hundred people for your product or service -- people that
you feel would be your ideal clients. Since you want them
to choose you and your business, let's have a look at the
likelihood that this will actually happen.[1]

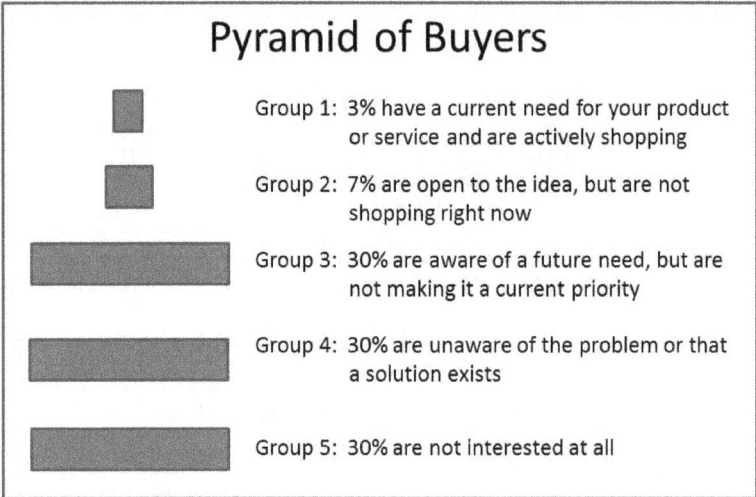

## Pyramid of Buyers

Group 1: 3% have a current need for your product or service and are actively shopping

Group 2: 7% are open to the idea, but are not shopping right now

Group 3: 30% are aware of a future need, but are not making it a current priority

Group 4: 30% are unaware of the problem or that a solution exists

Group 5: 30% are not interested at all

---

1 I first learned about the Pyramid of Buyers and the concept of
buying criteria from the Business Mastery Program created by the
late Chet Holmes. The diagram is my own interpretation.

In reality, only 3% of this group of one hundred people are actually looking for your product or service right now. They have a current need in their personal or work lives. They may be going through some sort of transition or they have a problem that needs solving. They are receptive to and ready to decide on a solution and – here's the key – they are *actively* out shopping now.

This is a very small group. Everyone wants their business, but don't forget that you're not the only one marketing to these 3%. Your competitors are also clamoring for their attention. It's a dog eat dog world.

So what now? Should you just continue to work harder to get your share of the 3%? How much harder will you have to work?

What about the other 97%? Are they a lost cause? No, there's hope – let's have a look at them.

The second group in the Pyramid of Buyers consists of 7% of your target market. These 7% are open to your product or service, but are not actively shopping right now. These people do have the problem you solve, but they have not yet made up their minds to go out and buy a solution. They're thinking about it.

Now we get into bigger numbers. The third group comprises 30% of your target market – people who are aware that sometime in the future they will need the solution you offer. They're procrastinating and haven't made it a priority yet, because there is nothing pushing them to make a decision right now.

The fourth group also consists of 30% of your target market. These people *should* be looking for your products or services, but are not aware they have a problem or that someone like you exists who can help them solve their problem. This group is not actively shopping for what you have to offer.

Now we come to the last group – the final 30%. This group is a pure "no". They may have the problem you solve but are not at all ready to look at a solution. They raise lots of objections such as time, money, energy, other commitments, and so on. They may even be enjoying the problem and are not motivated enough to do anything to turn the situation around. On the other hand, you may *think* they're ideal clients, but in truth, they may not have the problem you solve. One way or another, they're simply not interested.

## What's Your Approach?

Have you been spending your time trying to reach only 3% of people already looking for a solution? You're probably working awfully hard to get a piece of that 3%. It's easy to be discouraged when you and your competitors are all vying for the attention of this one tiny group.

So first of all, ignore the bottom 30%. No point in trying to convince people to buy your products and services if they are simply not interested. You'll be banging your head against the wall, resulting in frustration and disillusionment – not to mention a bad headache.

You'll have a much better chance of success if you target groups two, three, and four – the 67% that may just need a little education to motivate them to buy from you.

## So How Do You Educate Them?

Your book can educate them. Your book can open their eyes and help influence their buying decision, without any pressure. You can use the experience you have and the frequently asked questions you receive to educate them.

There are two steps here. First of all, educate by giving massive value. This approach is in line with a common networking mantra that you may be familiar with "give first – give value".

So, how do you give value or educate? Talk about real-life clients (without breaking any confidentiality issues, of course). People love hearing stories about others just like them. Then provide a few impactful statistics about the industry or results of scientific studies and their effect on your target market, if it's appropriate. It's important to discuss typical problems and highlight your approach to solving them. Positioning yourself and your business as having the solutions to clients' problems will show your prospects that you have your clients' best interests in mind. It gives them hope.

By the way, don't steal other people's ideas. You can use them, comment on them, and reinterpret them but always give credit where credit is due. There's one speaker/ marketer whose webinars and written materials include concepts I've learned elsewhere. She never gives credit to the original source, and I have to say it influences my decision-making regarding her products and services. Admit it even when you don't know who to credit.

What you don't want is for people to read your information and then just discard it. You want them to take action. So here's step two. Organize the material in such a way that it leads your prospects to the logical conclusion that they need what you have to offer *right now*. -- assuming that this is in line with your objective – and why wouldn't it be? (See the section on **Determining Your Objective** further ahead.)

## What Influences Your Prospects' Decision to Buy a Product or Service?

Unless you've done your homework, one of the key things that you probably don't know about your prospects involves their buying criteria. These are the factors that influence their decision-making. Let's look at a couple of examples.

### Example 1:  Buying a Car

Let's say you're in the market to buy yourself a new car. Let's also say, for a moment, that you're a 22-year-old single male. You won't be looking for the same things in a car as a 38-year-old married female with two children or as a 65-year-old retired male. Your buying criteria, or key influences that affect your decision, will be different from the buying criteria of these other people. Here are some of the factors that may affect someone's car-buying decision:

- price
- safety ratings
- sportiness
- sexiness
- handling
- options
- resale value
- insurance costs
- fuel efficiency

- environmental impact

- rebates

- financing options

You have priorities and a certain lifestyle, and as a result, some of the items on this list are going to be far more important to you than others.

Now, let's say for a moment that you're the 38-year-old married female with two children. If as you enter the car dealership, I come along and give you a report that talks at length about the poor economy, people losing their jobs, and the need to save money – and then goes on to list the insurance premiums for various cars and how the average owner can save money, you are now more likely to be looking for a car that will cost you less in insurance.

On the other hand, if before you go car-shopping, I give you a report on air pollution – what it does to our immune systems, how it makes us feel, childhood illness rates associated with polluted air, how what cars spew out contributes to people dying younger – and then goes on to describe the pollution control devices on a particular group of cars, you are now far more likely to look for a car that is more environmentally friendly and has an exhaust system that doesn't contribute to polluting the air you and your family breath.

**Example 2: Buying Pet Food**

Let's look at a second example. If you're a pet owner, pet food is on your shopping list fairly regularly. When you glance over the shelves in your local grocery store or pet shop, you're faced with a variety of pet food options.

How do you decide which pet food to buy? For some people, price is the deciding factor. Which pet food can they afford? Others make their choice based on health concerns. They look at the list of ingredients and rule out anything with additives in it. Still others make their selection based on taste (not theirs – their pets' taste). Which food wouldn't their cat or dog touch the last time they poured it into their pet's bowl?

Now, let's say I'm standing outside your favorite pet shop. Before you walk into the store, I engage you in conversation and hand you a report about the unhealthy hidden ingredients in pet food these days. You read the report, and begin to be aware of all the chemicals and unhealthy ingredients some companies are putting into your pet's food. You also read what these additives are doing to the health of this family member – impact on its coat or skin, increased chances of getting cancer, and so on.

Now, as you head down the pet food aisle, you are far more likely to read the labels and look for organic pet food. The report gave you value – educated you – but also influenced your buying criteria (the factors that you consider important when selecting a product or service). Your criteria became health. Importantly for the manufacturer of organic pet food, the report also positioned a purchase – gave the reader of the report good solid reasons to purchase their pet food.

Instead of giving you the report about unhealthy hidden ingredients in pet food, let's say I give you a report entitled "5 Ways Your Family is Flushing Money Down the Toilet". One of those 5 ways includes spending too much at the grocery store. The report describes a variety of ways to save money when shopping, including what you spend on pet food. Now as you make your way down the pet food aisle, you are almost certainly going to be focused on the price of pet food. The report influenced your buying criteria, and as a result, price became the most important factor for you. The report also positioned the purchase. In this scenario, if you're a manufacturer of low-priced pet food, you have a much better chance of getting the sale.

## Your Book Can Make the Difference

So, back to your book. Here's a great opportunity to educate your prospects (especially the 67% we talked about earlier – the 67% of your target market not actively shopping for what you have to offer right now but who can be influenced with a little bit of education). When you're pitching your products and services, your book and the position you take in educating your prospects could easily influence their buying criteria, and as a result, their buying decision – in your favor.

Needless to say, you want prospects to consider you and your business as the only choice when they are in the market for your product or service. Admittedly, your business is much more complicated than buying pet food. To give you some food for thought, here are a few other things that may influence your prospects' decision-making:

- reputation

- delivery time

- advertising

- weight or outward appearance of the product

- packaging and labels

- appearance and size of facilities

- time in business

- customer list (and testimonials)

- market share

- price (where price connotes quality)

- parent company identity (size, financial stability, etc.)[2]

You can easily include stories or other content in your book that illustrate some of these factors and help position your prospects' purchase in your favor. To simplify things for your reader, only choose those factors that differentiate you from your competitors.

---

2  Source: www.thebusinessowner.com

**Has your target market ever bought a product or service like yours before?**

Here's one final thought on this topic. Marketing guru Dan Kennedy teaches that it is always easier to sell your product or service to someone who has bought a similar product or service in the past (even if it was from a competitor). That's why he advocates doing the necessary research to find out this information and selecting these people as your target audience.

Along the way, you're going to meet people who fit into the various groups in the Buyer's Pyramid – and who may or may not have bought a similar product or service before. They're going to need some education in order to help them understand your particular product or service – who it is for, what problems it solves, and how it does it differently from others.

What better way to do it than through your book!

# Chapter 4:

# Getting Started on Your Book

We've spent a lot of time talking about the important marketing benefits that having your own business book will give you. In this chapter, we're going to start looking at the technical aspects of writing the book. Before you get down to the actual task of writing your book, there are a few decisions that you'll need to make first.

## Narrowing Down the Expertise You Want to Promote

There may be several areas or fields in which you have a lot of knowledge and experience. In order not to confuse your prospects and water down your value, you'll want to select only one of these areas to promote. Your credibility depends on exhibiting very clear expertise on one topic. For example, if you're a real estate agent and a mortgage broker, choose one of these topics for the book. You can always write another book later (creating a series – now you've got even more credibility).

## Selecting Your Target Market

You may already have a current client or patient base and want to continue working with the same types of client. From your experience working with them, you will already be familiar with their typical concerns and issues. If you're an accountant specializing in taxation, you already know the most common questions people ask. If you are a chiropractor, there are a number of questions that you repeatedly get concerning back care. If you're a divorce lawyer, you probably encounter a few standard situations regularly.

If your goal is to attract a new type of clientele or patient, you'll need to anticipate what their concerns and questions will be about what you do. These questions may very well be the same as the ones from your current client base, but it is wise to do some research on your planned target market.

If you're a realtor, will prospects who are trying to sell their million-dollar home have the same questions as those putting their $100,000 home up for sale? A bit of research will give you the answer.

(Refer to my earlier discussion about buyers in chapter 3.)

## Determining Your Objective

Your book must be client-centered. It's not about you. To truly be of service to your target market (remember the networking mantra "give first – give value"), you must keep in mind that although your book is a promotional tool, it must be all about "them" – the people in your target market – the problems they have, the questions they typically ask, the results they want.

Before you can even begin to write your book, you'll need to decide on your objective. How? By asking yourself this question:

> "What is it I want my readers to *do* by the time they've finished reading my book?"

Most writers have no idea how to answer this question. They feel driven to write – to record their thoughts and ideas or share their expertise. That's it. You, on the other hand, know by now that your book is your best business card, and that it has many marketing advantages for you and your business. That's why you're writing it.

You must have a clear objective or your book will be all over the place – and your readers will be confused. Here are some questions that will help you determine your overall objective. Do you want your readers to...

- be aware of or informed about your topic *only*? (Is that enough? How will that benefit your business?)
- be inspired, excited, and motivated to do something?
- perform differently at work, in their relationships, or in some other aspect of their lives?
- take a specific action, such as visit your website, call your office for a consultation, or buy your product or service?

Choose one or more – but choose! Once you're clear on the answer, and as a result clear on your objective, it will be easy for you to decide what you should put into your book. Your objective will also serve as your guide through all the decision-making regarding your book that is yet to come.

## Deciding on the Style of Your Book

There are a number of different styles or formats that are popular for business books. Your next task is to decide what format is suitable for showcasing your particular expertise and will best communicate what your prospects want to see and read.

- Does your information lend itself best to a step-by-step outline of your key points?

- Will a question and answer interview-style book help your prospects the most?

- How about a compiled list of items (e.g. top 10 ...) or collection of easily readable tips that can be scanned quickly?

- Is a photo book the best way to illustrate your expertise?

Since one of your goals should be to get the book out as quickly as possible, you don't want to spend a long time writing it. We're all about speed here. So choose a style that is easy for you to work with and to use as an organizational tool for your information.

# Chapter 5:

# Writing Your Book

Now that you've decided on your target market, what they want to know, and how they want to consume the information, you're ready to get down to actually writing your manuscript.

## Creating a Benefit-Oriented Title

You want to create a title that is appealing to your target market. As we discussed in the previous chapter, you have a really good idea of what your prospects want to know. Your title and subtitle should talk directly to those needs and wants. When you hand your book to prospects, you want them to identify with the title immediately. You also want them to have a strong emotional reaction that gets them so excited that they want to open the book immediately. Their gut reaction should be, "This book was written for me!"

Your title and subtitle should also reflect your authority and expertise – and help readers start get to know you and your business. You're selling without selling. If well written and edited, your book conveys the message that "This person really knows his/her stuff."

Your subtitle is as important as your title. The subtitle expands upon and completes the title, clearly establishing the value and benefits of what's inside. If you can, using a number in the subtitle helps define the value for the reader. It also assumes some sort of list and readers love lists.

Here are a few title/subtitle combinations (with and without numbers) to get you thinking about yours.

- It's in the Fine Print: 15 Little Known Facts About Insuring Your Home and Your Car
- Selling Your House: 40 Tips for Making Your House Irresistible to Buyers so You Can Sell it in 30 Days

- Is Your Dentist Right for You? The Top 5 Reasons for Choosing a Dentist Who Specializes in Treating Diabetic Patients

- After the Divorce: Advice on How to Make the Best Financial Decisions After a Devastating Divorce

- Save Your Back: How to Keep Your Back in Good Working Order

- Outsmarting the Tax Man: Tax Saving Advice for Singles

When creating your title and subtitle, remember what your purpose is. Here in this book, our purpose and our focus is on creating and publishing "your best business card" in order to stand out from your competition – to impress potential clients in your marketplace much more than an ordinary little business card can.

## Compiling the Content for Your Book

### The Interview Method

The interview method is an easy way to generate content if you don't have a lot of time to devote to the writing of your book. Typically an initial meeting with a potential client generates some of the most frequently asked questions (FAQs) you encounter on a regular basis. You can use these questions as the basis for an interview that generates the content for your book. Since you know your subject matter so well, answering these FAQs is easy for you.

You will really shine in the eyes of your prospects if you also include a section in your book of "should ask questions" (SAQs). People often don't know what questions they should be asking, what types of situations could arise, and how circumstances might affect them. As an expert, you can point out a few different examples. This shows that you have a depth and breadth of knowledge and experience that is truly impressive and helpful.

Once you have the answers to these FAQs and SAQs documented, you'll have the rough draft of your book. From there, it's just a case of organizing, editing, and polishing.

**Using Your Existing Materials**

If you write a business blog, newsletter, or series of articles on a regular basis, you already have content that can easily be compiled into a book. Even if you have articles sitting on your computer that have never been published or posted anywhere, you can certainly use them. You've already done a lot of the work! You've thought through the ideas and organized them into structured sentences and paragraphs. It shouldn't be too difficult to figure out what you might be missing and what you need to add.

The next step is easy – selecting those pieces that best meet your objective and address the needs of your potential clients, patients, or customers. The material you choose will probably need some editing and re-organization since the purpose of your book is narrower than that of your blog or newsletter.

One of my clients is an IT professional who has been writing a blog for the past few years. His blog posts now number over 450 and luckily he categorized and tagged them for easy retrieval. He has chosen the topic of his upcoming book and is in the process of sifting through and selecting the applicable articles. Next, he'll be grouping them according to sub-topics and eliminating any overlap or redundancy. Creating chapter titles will be easy since each post already has a heading and may just need a little tweaking.

## Creating a List

Luckily anything can be turned into a list – and any list can easily be converted into a book for publication, e.g. 35 Ways to…. 10 Things You Need to Know About….The Top 20 Reasons You Must….

If you decide to use the list approach, you'll find it easy to brainstorm, organize, and write your content very quickly. Lists allow you to chunk your information, suggestions, or advice down into bite-sized pieces, and that takes a lot of the stress out of writing. You can even use a simple formula to write each chunk. For example, you might decide to include

- a short introduction to the point
- the key point with appropriate details
- common issues or concerns
- an example or two
- a short conclusion

If you want to kick it up a notch, you could also add a chart, photo, quote, or statistic to each chunk. (Remember, my purpose throughout this book is to encourage you to get the book written as quickly as possible. So, don't spend too much time on adding in extras.) Once a chunk is complete, you move on to the next chunk – and the next and the next.

By the way, people love reading lists. They're easy to read and easy to follow. There's also a curiosity factor in that people are intrigued when they hear or read titles such as "21 Little-Known Facts About..." "15 Ways to..." They want to know more – and that means they'll read your book!

## Credibility Enhancers

The intent of your book, as we've talked about earlier, is to give value to your prospects and help them make a buying decision in your favor. On the one hand, you're trying to impress prospects and attract clients. On the other hand, you don't want to be too boastful and self-serving. Your readers will recognize and resent a self-centered approach.

That being said, here's a list of the types of things that will add to your credibility:

- credentials (degrees, diplomas, certifications)
- client stories (problems solved)

- additional training and education you've received

- nominations or awards received

- people you've worked with

- mentors you've had

- testimonials

- other publications (books, articles, etc.)

Some of the items on this list can be woven casually into your book through stories or examples. Others should be included on the "About the Author" page where they'll be more appropriate.

# Chapter 6:

# Preparing Your Book for Print Publication

In this chapter, we'll be looking at turning your manuscript into a soft cover book. This is where we move from the content to the technical details of getting a book published.

**Trim Size**

This is the first decision that needs to be made. Trim size refers to the dimensions of the book and governs the interior layout and exterior design.

## Interior Decisions

There are many details and decisions involved in completing the interior of the book. Included are additional content decisions, layout decisions, and even marketing-related decisions.

Your book will need certain front matter such as the title page, copyright page, disclaimers, dedications, table of contents, etc. Your book's content along with its chapter headings and subheadings will require stylizing. This includes selecting appropriate fonts and layout settings that make your book easy to navigate and easy to read.

Some of the items you'll want to include will support your marketing efforts, such as

- information about your products and services
- testimonials from satisfied clients
- your company website address
- your contact information

## Exterior Cover Design

As much as we hope that people don't judge a book by its cover, we know they do. They make snap judgments based on its title, subtitle, colors, font, graphics, and so on.

Is it appealing? Does it say "Open me. I've got great stuff inside." Although you have a captive audience to a certain degree (that is, most people will be receiving the book directly from you as opposed to choosing it from the many others on the virtual or physical bookshelf of their favorite bookstores), they can still decide to read it or not. You want it to be eye-catching.

A professional cover design is essential to ensuring that the expertise and work that you put into the interior of the book is not dismissed as amateurish and unprofessional even before people have a chance to look inside.

Your cover design must make a connection with your target audience in the same way that the title does. What would your prospects and clients expect of a book from someone in your profession? What should a book written by a real estate professional look like? What about a book written by a financial advisor, a dentist, a party planner, a cosmetician, or a carpet cleaner? You want your cover design to strike the right balance between attractiveness and relevance. A good graphic designer can do that for you.

## Publishing to Amazon's CreateSpace

One option that allows you to print only as many books as you want is Amazon's CreateSpace service. You don't need to fill your garage full of books. CreateSpace is a print-on-demand service for soft cover books that lets the author or publisher decide how many books to print at a time.

The first step is to create your free account at www.CreateSpace.com. Once you're in, you use your member dashboard to guide you through the necessary steps. You start by adding your new title, and then you follow the step-by-step process for uploading all the information necessary to publish your book.

You'll need to have the following things ready for upload:

- the correctly formatted interior of the book
- the artwork for the front cover in high resolution

- the back cover elements including your photo (optional) and a description of the book

If you don't have everything ready, then you can log out and come back later to finish the rest of the requirements. When everything is in place, you'll need to review the book. CreateSpace will let you know if there is anything missing.

Note: CreateSpace is set up for American residents but international folks can certainly publish to this platform as well. You must complete the information regarding how you would like to be paid when sales come in. Amazon is required to deduct a tax. If you are not a U.S. resident or citizen, I strongly suggest that you consult your accountant for advice on how to handle this tax situation.

## The Approval Process

There are several steps to the approval process.

You (the author and publisher) need to have a look at the final layout of the interior as well as the exterior (the front and back covers) to make sure everything is as you want it to be. Check all aspects of the book for errors. Check spelling, spacing, and so on. Although you can review the book online, you'll have a much better idea of the end result if you review a physical copy of the book. After all, do you really want to take a chance on ordering copies for distribution to prospects and clients only to find out when you receive them that there is a major problem with the book? If you can hold a sample in your hand, you'll know what it will feel like to someone else. You'll know its weight, size, and appearance. It will also be easier to go through the book with a fine tooth comb. You can use a highlighter and sticky notes to mark anything that needs editing or fixing.

Making a book available through Amazon requires their approval. Amazon wants to ensure that you have publishing rights to the material in your book and that all the technical specifications have been met. If you want to make your book available on Amazon in both soft cover and e-book versions, you'll need separate approvals. KDP (Kindle Direct Publishing) is the home for e-books whereas CreateSpace is for soft cover books. If the book is not approved, Amazon will specify what modifications are required. Once you make the changes, you'll need to resubmit the book for approval. Amazon will let you know when your book is live on its website.

You can order as many copies as you'd like to use for distribution to your prospects and clients and you can order more at any point in time.

**Other Options**

If you decide not to go the Amazon route, you can publish the book through other print-on-demand services or have a printing company print out a set quantity of books. Note that they may have other requirements for formatting and cover design that we haven't covered here.

# Chapter 7:

# Your Next Step

So now you know the benefits and marketing advantages of having your very own business book and why it really is your best business card. You also know what you need to do in order to write and publish your book.

As I see it, you have four options.

The first, of course, is to do nothing. You can continue fighting the competition using your 2 x 3 ½ inch business card and get the same results.

The second option is for you to personally work through the lengthy learning curve and try to do all the writing, editing, graphic design, formatting, publishing, and uploading yourself, but consider this:

- How long will it take for you to learn all the steps involved in writing and publishing your book?

- How much time are you going to save if you hire Lindmaur Publishing to take care of it for you? (After all, your expertise lies elsewhere, not in creating and publishing books – right?)

- How long will it take you to produce a book without access to the systems that we use?

- How much time would it take even if you had access to our systems?

- How much is your time worth?

The third option is to take care of some of the steps in creating your book yourself and have Lindmaur Publishing handle the rest. (e.g. You may already have a manuscript but require formatting and print publication.)

The fourth option is to let Lindmaur Publishing take care of the entire process for you while you go about the business of earning money in your area of expertise. We'll need some input from you, but after that our team can do the rest. Before you know it, you'll have your book in hand ready to give out to prospects and clients.

## Our Services

We'd be delighted to work with you in getting your business book published!

Go to **http://www.YourBestBusinessCard.info** for more on how you can become a published author and stand out from your competition.

# About the Author

Ida Shessel has been a professional speaker, author, and workshop leader for over 30 years helping individuals and corporate teams enhance their communication, training, and presentation skills.

It has been Ida's ongoing mission to engage, encourage, and most importantly to empower people to acquire the skills they need to help their organizations and businesses thrive. She has worked with leading organizations in the fields of technology, finance, pharmaceuticals, government, automotive, telecommunications, gaming, retail, higher education, and more.

Ida is the author of five business books, two blogs, and numerous articles and tips booklets. In *Your Best Business Card: How to Stand Out from the Competition with Your Very*

*Own Book*, Ida shares her love of writing and publishing books in order to once again empower others.

She earned her B.Sc. in Psychology from the University of Toronto and her M.Ed. in Adult Education from the Ontario Institute for Education. Ida lives in Toronto, Canada.

# Testimonials

"Working with Ida has been wonderful. Her understanding of the publishing process combined with her insights as an author enabled me to easily convert my blog into a manuscript and prepare it for publication."

E. Kochman, President, Optimal Upgrade Consulting Inc.

"For years I've wanted to write a book about my work in wellness and Traditional Chinese Medicine. I didn't know how to get started, but Ida has been very helpful in getting my information into book form. She's easy to work with and I would definitely recommend her publishing services to anyone who wants to get their business book done quickly."

May Hao, Director, Life Vitality Wellness Centre

# Other Books by Ida Shessel

## Communicate Like a Top Leader: 64 Strategies Top Leaders Use to Engage, Encourage, and Empower Others

ISBN: 978–0–987-9339–0–4 (hardcover)

ISBN: 978–0–987-9339–1-1 (ebook)

Leading people is an awesome responsibility – and communicating effectively with them can be challenging. Communicate Like a Top Leader focuses on overcoming 8 typical communication challenges using strategies that engage, encourage, and empower others.

"What a wonderful book! It is loaded with wonderful ways to bring out the best in each person."

Brian Tracy, Author, Full Engagement, www.briantracy.com

"If you're ready to grow yourself and your organization at a rapid rate, then read, absorb and use the strategies in this

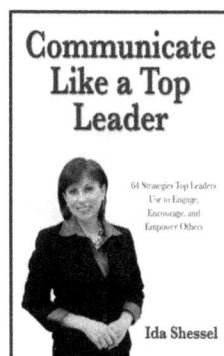

brilliant book by my friend Ida Shessel. Then do yourself a huge favor and hire her for presentation skills workshops and coaching. You'll be so grateful you did!"

James Malinchak, Featured on ABC's Hit TV Show "Secret Millionaire", Founder, www.BigMoneySpeaker.com

## The Expert's Guide to Engaging, Encouraging, and Empowering for Profit: The Simple and Easy-To-Follow System for Getting Paid What You're Worth

ISBN: 978–09879339–7–3 (paperback)

Do you have expertise, knowledge, and skills that others want and need?

The good news is that you can turn that expertise into a profitable income stream. You can train and coach others – be appreciated, sought after, and in demand for what you have to offer – and get well paid for it. In The Expert's Road Map to Engaging, Encouraging, and Empowering for Profit, you'll learn valuable insights, tips, and information that can be used to turn your knowledge into consulting and training services for clients around the world – whether it's face-to-face, ear-to-ear, or online.

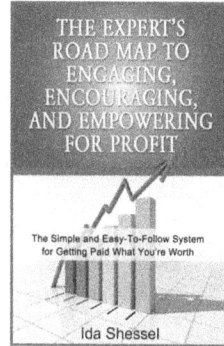

## Improving Memory: Easy Tips for Improving Your Memory at Work

ISBN: 978–0–9879339–4–2 (e-book)

ISBN: 978–09879339–5–9 (paperback)

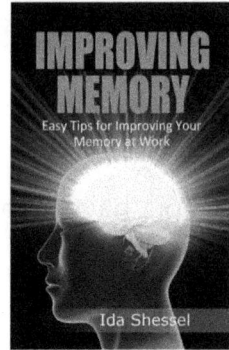

This book has been written so that you can consume it in bite-sized pieces. Just pick a tip and incorporate it into your life. Memory tips are transferable, so feel free to use them every day and share them with your colleagues, friends, and family.

Discover

- the secret to a great memory
- 10 benefits that a good memory can provide on the job
- 10 effective ways to remember names and faces
- 16 easy techniques and games for improving memory
- tips on choosing memory programs and online games
- 11 more helpful tips on memory enhancement

- 10 top memory-boosting foods
- 6 alertness saboteurs

"This is an easy, informative ready that helps you incorporate practical ways of boosting your memory skills. With the built-in links it is easy to garner additional information about supporting your memory and....remember them!"

Constance G.

## Meeting with Success: Tips and Techniques for Great Meetings

ISBN: 978–1–6897326–15–2

(paperback)

Turn ordinary discussions into focused, energetic sessions that produce positive results. If you are a meeting leader or a participant who is looking for ways to get more out of every meeting you lead or attend, then this book is for you. It's filled with practical tips and techniques to help you improve your meetings. You'll learn to spot the common problems and complaints that spell meeting disaster, how people who are game players can effect your meeting, fool-proof methods to motivate and inspire, and templates that show you how to achieve results. Learn to cope with annoying meeting situations, including problematic participants, and run focused, productive meetings.

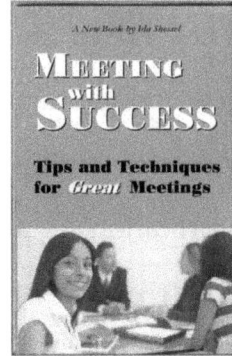

Go to http://lindmaurpublishing.com/?p=62 for a full list of books by Ida Shessel.

www.ingramcontent.com/pod-product-compliance
Lightning Source LLC
Chambersburg PA
CBHW060648210326
41520CB00010B/1782